Pod and Pot

Sounds Easy Series

ISBN 0 905858 73 5

Designed by Howard Birkett,
Amaryllis Software Ltd, Berkhamsted, Herts

Printed by Streetsprinters, Baldock, Herts

Published by
Egon Publishers Ltd
Royston Road, Baldock, Herts SG7 6NW

TEACHERS' NOTES

LEVEL 0. PRE-READING BOOKS

These books have been designed to help children with visual sequential memory difficulties. They draw attention to the vowels 'a', 'o', 'i', 'e' and 'u' (in that order). First say the word to the pupil and talk about the picture. The pupil should then trace each letter with a finger, saying the letter sound at the same time and finally say the whole word. Point out the highlighted vowel.

INTRODUCTORY LEVEL AND LEVEL 1. FIRST READING BOOKS

Can be used as a reading scheme, or as supplementary books to Spelling Made Easy, 'Fat Sam' - Introductory Level and 'Sam and the Tramp' - Level 1 (Violet Brand). They gradually introduce new vowel sounds, reinforcing the word families.

Acknowledgements

Special thanks to John and Heather Adkins, the staff and children of Egerton-Rothesay Lower School, Berkhamsted, to Violet Brand for her encouragement and inspiration and of course to my family, Lucy (for Ted), Joanna (for Top the Frog) and my husband Howard, without whom these books would not have been written.

Pod and Pot

ROSALIND BIRKETT

Introductory Level Book 4

Sounds Easy Series

EPL

EGON PUBLISHERS LTD

Pot and Pod in the sun.
Pod and Pot get hot in
the sun. Pod fans Pot and
Pot fans Pod.

Pod and Pot can run. Pod and Pot run up the hill to Ted's hut. Ed is at Ted's hut with Ted.

Ted and Ed let Pot and Pod in. Ted gets Pod and Pot eggs and jam buns. The pals sit on Ted's red rug. It is fun.

The pals set off to get wet in the pond. It is fun in the pond and not hot. Ed has a big net and Pod and Pot dig.

Pot hits a tin and tugs at it. Pod tugs with Pot, tug, tug, tug. Ted tugs with Pod and Pot, tug, tug, tug. Ed tugs with Ted and Pod and Pot, tug, tug, tug. Up pops the big tin.

Pod and Pot, Ed and Ted are glad. It is a big wet, red tin. Pot tugs at the lid.

In the tin is a big cup. Ted is glad. Ted had lost this cup. Ted hugs Pot and Pod and Ed.